A LIFEGUIDE 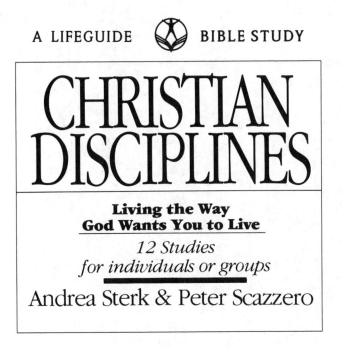 BIBLE STUDY

CHRISTIAN DISCIPLINES

**Living the Way
God Wants You to Live**

*12 Studies
for individuals or groups*

Andrea Sterk & Peter Scazzero

With Notes for Leaders

D0168325

INTERVARSITY PRESS
DOWNERS GROVE, ILLINOIS 60515

©1985 by InterVarsity Christian Fellowship of the United States of America

All rights reserved. No part of this book may be reproduced in any form without written permission from InterVarsity Press, P.O. Box 1400, Downers Grove, IL 60515.

InterVarsity Press® is the book-publishing division of InterVarsity Christian Fellowship®, a student movement active on campus at hundreds of universities, colleges and schools of nursing in the United States of America, and a member movement of the International Fellowship of Evangelical Students. For information about local and regional activities, write Public Relations Dept., InterVarsity Christian Fellowship, 6400 Schroeder Rd., P.O. Box 7895, Madison, WI 53707-7895.

LifeGuide® is a registered trademark of InterVarsity Christian Fellowship.

All Scripture quotations, unless otherwise indicated, are taken from the HOLY BIBLE, NEW INTERNATIONAL VERSION®. NIV®. Copyright ©1973, 1978, 1984 by International Bible Society. Used by permission of Zondervan Publishing House. All rights reserved.

Cover photograph: Peter French

ISBN 0-8308-1055-2

Printed in the United States of America ∞

21	20	19	18	17	30	29	28	27	26	25	24	23	22	21	20	19	18	17
11	10	09	08	07	06	05	04	03	02	01	00	99	98	97	96	95	94	

Contents

FASTING

Getting the Most
from LifeGuide Bible Studies

Many of us long to fill our minds and our lives with Scripture. We desire to be transformed by its message. LifeGuide Bible Studies are designed to be an exciting and challenging way to do just that. They help us to be guided by God's Word in every area of life.

How They Work

LifeGuides have a number of distinctive features. Perhaps the most important is that they are *inductive* rather than *deductive*. In other words, they lead us to *discover* what the Bible says rather than simply *telling* us what it says.

They are also thought provoking. They help us to think about the meaning of the passage so that we can truly understand what the author is saying. The questions require more than one-word answers.

The studies are personal. Questions expose us to the promises, assurances, exhortations and challenges of God's Word. They are designed to allow the Scriptures to renew our minds so that we can be transformed by the Spirit of God. This is the ultimate goal of all Bible study.

The studies are versatile. They are designed for student, neighborhood and church groups. They are also effective for individual study.

How They're Put Together

LifeGuides also have a distinctive format. Each study need take no more than forty-five minutes in a group setting or thirty minutes in personal study— unless you choose to take more time.

The studies can be used within a quarter system in a church and fit well in a semester or trimester system on a college campus. If a guide has more than thirteen studies, it is divided into two or occasionally three parts of approximately twelve studies each.

LifeGuides use a workbook format. Space is provided for writing answers to each question. This is ideal for personal study and allows group members to prepare in advance for the discussion.

The studies also contain leader's notes. They show how to lead a group discussion, provide additional background information on certain questions, give helpful tips on group dynamics and suggest ways to deal with problems which may arise during the discussion. With such helps, someone with little or no experience can lead an effective study.

Suggestions for Individual Study

1. As you begin each study, pray that God will help you to understand and apply the passage to your life.

2. Read and reread the assigned Bible passage to familiarize yourself with what the author is saying. In the case of book studies, you may want to read through the entire book prior to the first study. This will give you a helpful overview of its contents.

3. A good modern translation of the Bible, rather than the King James Version or a paraphrase, will give you the most help. The New International Version, the New American Standard Bible and the Revised Standard Version are all recommended. However, the questions in this guide are based on the New International Version.

4. Write your answers in the space provided in the study guide. This will help you to express your understanding of the passage clearly.

5. It might be good to have a Bible dictionary handy. Use it to look up any unfamiliar words, names or places.

Suggestions for Group Study

1. Come to the study prepared. Follow the suggestions for individual study mentioned above. You will find that careful preparation will greatly enrich your time spent in group discussion.

2. Be willing to participate in the discussion. The leader of your group will not be lecturing. Instead, he or she will be encouraging the members of the group to discuss what they have learned from the passage. The leader will be asking the questions that are found in this guide. Plan to share what God has taught you in your individual study.

3. Stick to the passage being studied. Your answers should be based on the verses which are the focus of the discussion and not on outside authorities such as commentaries or speakers. This guide deliberately avoids jumping

from book to book or passage to passage. Each study focuses on only one passage. Book studies are generally designed to lead you through the book in the order in which it was written. This will help you follow the author's argument.

4. Be sensitive to the other members of the group. Listen attentively when they share what they have learned. You may be surprised by their insights! Link what you say to the comments of others so the group stays on the topic. Also, be affirming whenever you can. This will encourage some of the more hesitant members of the group to participate.

5. Be careful not to dominate the discussion. We are sometimes so eager to share what we have learned that we leave too little opportunity for others to respond. By all means participate! But allow others to also.

6. Expect God to teach you through the passage being discussed and through the other members of the group. Pray that you will have an enjoyable and profitable time together.

7. If you are the discussion leader, you will find additional suggestions and helpful ideas for each study in the leader's notes. These are found at the back of the guide.

Introducing Christian Disciplines

Fast-food restaurants. Rapid weight-loss diets. Instant 24-hour banking. Getting rich quick. Today's society looks for instant gratification and results. More. Better. Quicker. Richer. Often the values of society shape our view of discipleship. We demand instant godliness, overnight "success" in the Christian life. As a result we end up discouraged and frustrated by the shallowness of our walk with God. Richard Foster spells out our dilemma: "Superficiality is the curse of our age. The doctrine of instant gratification is a primary spiritual problem. The desperate need today is not for a greater number of intelligent people, or gifted people, but for deep people" (*Celebration of Discipline* [New York: Harper & Row, 1978], p. 1).

Christian Disciplines is designed to strengthen your foundations in Christ and deepen your relationship with him. We have prepared twelve inductive Bible studies which will help you grapple with the basic disciplines of the Christian life. *Discipline* is not a very popular word today. We tend to think only of its negative connotations—of rules, punishment, limitations on our freedom, and legalism. We have somehow lost the positive biblical emphasis on discipline which leads to freedom and joy in the Holy Spirit. Paul's instruction to Timothy reminds us of the importance and value of a disciplined life: "Train yourself to be godly. For physical training is of some value, but godliness has value for all things, holding promise for both the present life and the life to come" (1 Tim 4:7-8).

While dealing with the foundational disciplines of the faith, we have also sought to cover a wider range of topics which are crucial for the body of Christ in this generation: missions, crosscultural ministry, social justice, and managing time and gifts. Although the studies in this guide are arranged in a particular sequence, please feel free to change the order to meet your needs.

Our prayer is that in the midst of a turbulent world, God will use this guide to establish you in his truth so that the Lord Jesus may commend you as he did the church at Thyatira: "I know your deeds, your love and faith, your service and perseverance, and that you are now doing more than you did at first" (Rev 2:19). May God keep us from complacency, and may we press on to know him more deeply and obey him more fully!

1
Quiet
Time

Exodus 33:7–34:10, 27-35

W hen we really want to get to know someone, there is no substitute for spending quality time together. The same is true of our relationship with God. Throughout the Gospels we see that Jesus placed a high priority on being alone with his Father. Despite the overwhelming demands on his time, "Jesus often withdrew to lonely places and prayed" (Lk 5:16). This discipline can be seen in the lives of the great men and women of the Old Testament as well. Moses was one such person.

Returning from Mount Sinai, Moses finds the people of Israel worshiping a golden calf. He is infuriated, yet he intercedes before the Lord for his people. While we will probably never spend forty days and nights alone with God, Moses' heart for God and time in his presence is a good example of what a quiet time is all about.

---

1. Spending time regularly with God is difficult for many people. What are some of the reasons for this?

BUSY SCHEDULES   OTHER GODS
PEOPLE DON'T KNOW HIM
DISTRACTIONS

---

2. Read Exodus 33:7-23. What do we learn about the purpose of the "tent of meeting" in verses 7-11?

FACE TO FACE COMMUNICATION c̄ GOD
TALKING c̄ A FRIEND
A TIME OF UNDISTURBANCE

3. Describe Moses' relationship with God as depicted in these verses.

FRANK, FORTHRIGHT, BOLD, HONEST

4. In verses 12-23 we are allowed inside the tent of meeting while Moses converses with God. What requests does Moses make in verses 13, 15 and 18?

13 "TEACH ME YOUR WAYS" REMEMBER THE NATION

15. DON'T SEND US ALONE

18. SHOW US YOUR GREATNESS

What seems to be his overriding desire?

TO GET TO KNOW GOD BETTER
TO GET CLOSER TO GOD

5. How does your desire to know God compare with Moses'?

IT PALES IF I DESIRED IT, I WOULD PUT IT INTO ACTION MORE OFTEN

6. Read 34:1-10. In verses 1-3 what commands does God give to Moses?

CHISEL OUT TWO TABLETS
BE READY IN THE MORNING
COME TO MT. SINAI
NO ONE IS TO COME c̄ YOU

7. Why do you think God demands that Moses come to him alone, apart from "even the flocks and herds" (v. 3)?

NO DISTRACTIONS, FOCUSED

How might Moses' example relate to our meeting with God?

A PLACE OF UNDISTURBANCE
BE READY / BE PREPARED

8. What distractions hinder you from spending quality time alone with the Lord?

T.V.
BOOKS
WORK
THOUGHTS

9. In verses 4-5 Moses carefully obeys God's commands, and the Lord reveals himself to him. What does Moses learn of God's character (vv. 6-7)?

LORD x2
COMPASSIONATE   *JUST*
GRACIOUSNESS
SLOW TO ANGER
ABOUNDING IN LOVE & FAITHFULNESS

10. What else do we observe about how Moses spent time with God (vv. 8-10)?

HUMBLE & LIFTED UP
POSTURE
ASKING FORGIVENESS
OFFERING AS SELF

11. Read 34:27-35. In these verses we see the conclusion of Moses' time with God and some of the results of that time. How are the Ten Commandments (v. 28) a partial fulfillment of Moses' request in 33:13?

SHOWS VIRTUES OF GOD

12. In verses 29-35 Moses comes down from Mount Sinai and returns to the camp. How was he affected by his time in God's presence?

RADIANCE
CHANGED WITHIN

---

13. In what ways can we expect to be changed by our times alone with God?

DIFFERENT PERSPECTIVE

---

14. In many ways Moses' experiences with God were unique and unrepeatable. Yet what practical help for our own quiet times can we derive from these chapters?

2
Prayer
Nehemiah 1:1—2:10

Alack of time or quality in prayer seems to be an almost universal frustration among Christians. A recent survey of American pastors revealed that the average pastor spends only three minutes a day in personal prayer. Andrew Murray once said that we spend a lifetime with Christ in the school of prayer. Yet too many of us are still in kindergarten!

Nehemiah provides an excellent model for Christians in the twentieth century. In the midst of daily pressures and crises, he demonstrates a life of deep dependence on God combined with well-planned action. During the exile Nehemiah served as cupbearer to the Persian king, Artaxerxes I (465-425 B.C.). To the Jewish people of that day the physical condition of Jerusalem (in this case the wall) was symbolic of the state of their relationship with God.

---

1. How do you usually respond to crises in your life?

BRINGS GREATER DEPENDENCE UPON GOD

---

2. Read Nehemiah 1:1—2:10. What tragic report does Hanani bring to Nehemiah about the Jewish remnant in Jerusalem (vv. 1-3)?

IN GREAT TROUBLE & DISGRACE
WALL BROKEN DOWN & GATES BURNED

3. In verse 4 there are several verbs which demonstrate Nehemiah's distress over Jerusalem's ruin. What do these verbs indicate about Nehemiah's heart and attitude toward God?

INCLINED TOWARDS GOD
BELIEVED GOD WOULD HEAR HIM
FELT WHAT GOD FELT

4. What does Nehemiah recognize about God's character in verse 5?

GREAT & FAITHFUL

How would this be an encouragement to him in prayer?

KNOWS GOD WOULD LISTEN & HEAR HIS PRAYS. FAITHFUL ANSWER & KEEP HIS WORD

5. What does Nehemiah's confession reveal about his character and his understanding of sin (vv. 6-7)?

HONEST TO LOOK AT HIS SIN SIN IS NOT AN ISOLATED ACT, BUT AGAINST THE VERY NATURE OF GOD

6. In verses 8-11, how does Nehemiah apply God's Word in his prayer?

MAKES APPLICATION BY QUOTING & APPLYING IT TO HIS PRESENT SITUATION

7. Think of people and things you pray for regularly. How can God's Word encourage you as you pray?

REMIND ME OF GOD'S INFINITE WISDOM & PLAN, HIS POWER & PROMISES

PARABLE OF JUDGE & PERSISTENT WIDOW

Prayer   **15**

8. The acrostic ACCTS (adoration, confession, consecration, thanksgiving, supplication) is a helpful reminder of the elements of a balanced prayer life. Which of these elements do you find in Nehemiah's prayer?

ADORATION
CONFESSION
CONSECRATION
SUPPLICATION

9. Which of these elements do you tend to omit when you pray, and why?

CONFESSION — UNCOMFORTABLE
CONSECRATION — FEAR OF WHAT GOD
MIGHT ASK

10. What impresses you about the discussion between Nehemiah and the king (2:1-4)?

BOLDNESS IN DISPLAYING EMOTION & THEN TALKING ABOUT IT

11. At the critical moment Nehemiah sends a brief "holy telegram" (v. 4). How can this little prayer also be a model for us?

LEARN TO RELY UPON GOD'S GUIDANCE IN THOSE CRITICAL MOMENTS

12. How does Nehemiah demonstrate a willingness to be used by God in answering his own prayers (vv. 1-10)?

STEPS OUT IN FAITH... ACTION

13. Summarize what we learned about the quality of Nehemiah's prayer life.

NATURAL RELIANCE UPON GOD BASED UPON HIS KNOWLEDGE OF GOD'S NATURE

14. In what areas do you most need to follow Nehemiah's example of prayer?

CONSISTENCY
NATURALNESS
ACTION

3
Bible
Study

2 Kings 22:1—23:7, 21-25

The Bible has transformed more lives than any book in the history of the world. It has shaped the course of Western civilization. Even amid rising secularism its indelible imprint remains.

In 2 Kings 22—23:30 Josiah and the nation of Israel experienced the transforming power of the Word of God. For fifty-seven years prior to King Josiah's reign, the Book of the Law (the Scriptures) had been neglected. Spiritually, the nation of Israel was in shambles.

1. Imagine that all the Bibles on earth were destroyed one hundred years ago. How might your life be different than it is now?

2. Read 2 Kings 22. Why does King Josiah send his secretary, Shaphan, to the temple of the Lord (vv. 3-7)?

3. Why is it ironic that the Book of the Law is found during temple repairs (vv. 8-10)?

In what ways are we guilty of engaging in a flurry of religious activities while neglecting God's Word?

4. How does Josiah respond when he hears the words of the Book of the Law (vv. 11-13)?

5. How does Huldah's prophecy summarize the two attitudes we can have toward God's Word (vv. 14-20)?

What are the ultimate consequences of these attitudes?

6. Read 23:1-7. What do we learn in verses 1-3 about Josiah's commitment to the Scriptures?

7. Describe the condition of the temple before Josiah's reforms (vv. 4-7).

What does the condition of the temple reveal about what happens when we neglect God's Word?

8. How does Josiah's commitment to the Scriptures affect the nation of Judah (vv. 4-7)?

9. Read 23:21-25. Compare your attitude and obedience to God's Word with Josiah's.

10. If you had Josiah's commitment to Scripture, how might your life be different?

11. How can we allow God's Word to have a greater impact on our lives?

4
Evangelism

Acts 17

Becky Pippert aptly observes that "there is one thing Christians and non-Christians have in common. They're both uptight about evangelism!" Even the great apostle Paul, whom we tend to think of as a relentless and fearless evangelist, reminded the Corinthians that he came to them "in weakness and fear, and with much trembling" (1 Cor 2:3). In fact, some members of the church remarked, "His letters are weighty and forceful, but in person he is unimpressive and his speaking amounts to nothing" (2 Cor 10:10). Yet we have much to learn from the example of Paul as one who in the power of the Holy Spirit and with deep conviction preached the good news of Jesus.

1. What are some of your feelings and struggles as you share the gospel with others?

2. Read Acts 17, observing how Paul's presentation of the gospel differed in each of the three cities he visited. Briefly describe any similarities and differences you notice.

3. If there was a synagogue in a city, Paul's custom was to go there first (v. 2). Why would this have been an effective strategy (vv. 1-4)?

4. Where could we go today to find people with religious interests?

As was the case with Paul (vv. 5-9), why might such people also be our most vigorous opponents?

5. In Thessalonica and Berea, Paul "reasoned with them from the Scriptures." In Athens he did not. When is it most effective to use the Bible as the basis for our evangelism?

6. Considering the hostility Paul faced in Thessalonica and Berea, and the fact that he was alone when he entered the pagan city of Athens (v. 16), how do you think Paul felt as he began to preach the gospel in Athens?

7. What drove Paul to preach the gospel despite his weakness (vv. 3, 16, 31)?

8. In Athens Paul not only preached in the synagogue but also in the marketplace (v. 17). Using your imagination and the information in verses 17-21, describe the people, sights and sounds of the marketplace.

9. Why would it be a logical place for Paul to go?

10. Where are the gathering places "pagans" go to today?

11. Study Paul's presentation of the gospel (vv. 22-31). How does he adapt his presentation to the interests and background of his audience?

How might we follow his example today without distorting the essential message of the gospel?

12. Compare and contrast the responses to the gospel in Thessalonica, Berea and Athens.

13. Bearing in mind that Paul's situations in this passage may differ considerably from your own, what can you learn from him about principles of evangelism?

5
Social
Justice

Amos 5:4—6:7

I used to think, when I was a child, that Christ might have been exaggerating when he warned about the dangers of wealth. Today I know better. I know how very hard it is to be rich and still keep the milk of human kindness. Money has a dangerous way of putting scales on one's eyes, a dangerous way of freezing people's hands, eyes, lips, and hearts."[1]

Israel in the eighth century B.C. was extremely prosperous and outwardly religious. An uneven distribution of wealth resulted in an immense chasm between the rich, bent on increasing their wealth, and the oppressed poor. Although externally devout, the nation was morally decadent. In the midst of this society God called out a shepherd and tender of sycamore-fig trees, a job reserved only for those at the bottom of the social ladder. He had no formal religious training or position. During the reign of Jeroboam II, around 760 B.C., this man, Amos, appeared on the scene. Speaking to a world not unlike our own, his message needs to be heard and obeyed in our day.

1. How can money or possessions tempt us toward insensitivity or compromise?

2. Read Amos 5:4-17. Bethel, Gilgal and Beersheba were centers of idolatry during the time of Amos. What do verses 4-6 reveal about the consequences of idolatry?

3. How can idolatry—both ancient and modern—lead to injustice and un-righteousness (v. 7)?

4. How would the Lord's description of himself (vv. 8-9) cause Israel to fear his judgment?

5. What forms did injustice and oppression take in Israel (vv. 10-13)?

In what specific ways are they manifested in our society?

6. How do the exhortations "Seek me" (v. 4), "Seek the LORD" (v. 6) and "Seek good" (v. 14) provide the remedy for idolatry and injustice?

7. If Israel failed to heed these exhortations, God warned that he would pass through their midst in judgment (vv. 16-17). In what sense is this warning applicable today?

8. Read 5:18—6:7. Describe the religious atmosphere and practices of the day (5:18-27).

In what ways were these attitudes and actions commendable?

9. Contemporary Christianity has been described as "privately engaging but socially irrelevant." Do you agree or disagree with this statement? Explain.

10. How might leisure, luxury and prestige lead to the sins described in 6:1-7?

In what ways are you guilty of similar sins?

11. There are many areas of social injustice today: lack of concern for the poor and needy, racism, wasteful lifestyle, neglect of the plight of the cities, political injustice and so on. In what area do you most need to change your attitude or lifestyle to reflect God's concern for justice and mercy?

¹Dom Helder Camara, *Revolution through Peace* (New York: Harper & Row, 1971), p. 142.

6
The
Church

Ephesians 4:1-16

Everyone is talking about the church. How does a church grow? What is the biblical structure for the church? What is the role of spiritual gifts in the body? How can we build biblical fellowship? How can the church be prophetic in our society? Books and articles addressing these and related issues have flooded the market in recent years. But perhaps the greatest need of the church today is to come to a renewed understanding of its own identity as the people of God. The book of Ephesians speaks to the crucial question of the nature and function of the church.

1. What has helped your church or fellowship group the most in promoting unity?

2. Read Ephesians 4:1-16. Identify and briefly comment on the qualities Paul urges us to exemplify in our relationships (vv. 1-3).

3. William Barclay depicts the relationship between first-century Jews and Gentiles as follows: "The Jews had an immense contempt for the Gentiles and considered them as 'created by God to be fuel for the fires of hell.' "¹ Against this background, describe the difficulties Jewish and Gentile Christians would face in seeking to maintain unity.

What similar tensions in the church today make it difficult to "keep the unity of the Spirit through the bond of peace"?

4. How can Paul's description of the body of Christ, the church, motivate us to live in unity (vv. 4-6)?

5. Verses 7-10 describe Christ as a triumphant conqueror who distributes gifts, the spoils of victory, to his people. What is the nature and purpose of the gifts Christ has given to the church (vv. 11-13)?

6. For many Christians, church is simply a place to sit under the ministry of gifted individuals (v. 11). How is this concept a distortion of our role as God's people (vv. 12-13)?

7. What is God's goal for the church according to verses 13-16?

8. What are the differences between spiritual infancy and spiritual maturity (vv. 13-16)?

9. What winds and waves are blowing and tossing the church today (v. 14)?

10. Why are spiritually mature Christians better able to withstand false teaching and "the cunning and craftiness of men in their deceitful scheming" (v. 14)?

11. Why is the balance of truth and love so essential as we seek to help others grow in Christ (v. 15)?

12. Paul mentions that each part must do its work in order for the body to grow and build itself up in love (v. 16). What work has God called you to do at the present time?

13. How has this passage helped you to understand the nature and purpose of a healthy church?

14. How has it helped you to better understand your own place in the church?

¹William Barclay, *Daily Bible Study,* p. 125.

7
Missions/ Crosscultural Ministry

Acts 10

Missions is a major theme of the Bible, running from Genesis to Revelation. The desire to see the gospel penetrate every culture and nation is at the very heart of God. Yet there is a tendency in our churches and personal lives to place it at the bottom of our agenda, especially when other concerns press upon our already overcrowded schedule. There is an urgent need to regain the biblical vision to see "every tongue confess that Jesus Christ is Lord, to the glory of God the Father" (Phil 2:11).

1. What keeps missions from being more important to most of us?

2. Read Acts 10:1-23. What do we learn about Cornelius in verses 1-7?

3. Imagine yourself in Peter's situation, having been taught from childhood that certain animals were unclean and not to be eaten. How might you respond to his vision (vv. 9-16)?

4. Why do you suppose the vision occurred three times?

5. In what additional ways did God's will become clearer to Peter (vv. 17-23)?

6. Read verses 23-48. How did Peter's vision break down his cultural resistance and prepare him for the meeting with Cornelius (vv. 23-29)?

7. The Jews viewed the Gentiles as unclean. What racial, cultural or economic groups have we tended to view with contempt?

What factors have led to this prejudice?

8. Verse 29 indicates that Peter still did not grasp why God sent him to Cornelius. What did Peter learn about the nature of the gospel through his encounter with this Gentile (vv. 30-35)?

9. How are verses 36-43 a fulfillment of Christ's statement, "You will be my witnesses in Jerusalem, and in all Judea and Samaria, and to the ends of the earth" (Acts 1:8)?

10. In spite of all that had happened, Peter and the Jews evidently assumed that the Gentiles would be second-class citizens. How did God convince them otherwise (vv. 44-48)?

11. Describe some of the cultural barriers around you.

12. How can you begin to penetrate these barriers with the gospel?

13. There are an estimated 4.5 billion people in the world today. At least 2.7

billion have never heard the gospel. Of this 2.7 billion an estimated 98% live outside of North America. Considering God's concern for the world and the present situation, what are the implications of these facts for: (a) the church worldwide and (b) your local church or fellowship group?

14. What are some ways you can become involved in the advancement of the gospel worldwide?

15. Spend time praying for missionaries you know.

8
Managing Time and Gifts

Matthew 25:14-30

Time is one of the most precious commodities in today's world. We always seem to suffer from a lack of it. In light of Christ's lordship the effective management of our time and gifts is absolutely crucial. Oswald Sanders wrote:

> After making a generous allowance of eight hours a day for sleep and rest—and few really need more than that—three hours a day for meals and social intercourse, ten hours a day for work and travel on five days, there still remain no fewer than thirty-five hours unaccounted for in each week. What happens to them? How are the extra two days in the week invested? The whole of a man's contribution to the kingdom of God might well turn upon how these crucial hours are employed. They will determine whether his life will be commonplace or extraordinary.[1]

Jesus addresses the seriousness of this issue in the Parable of the Talents.

1. What activities and responsibilities compete the most for your time?

2. Read Matthew 25:14-30. What arrangements does the master make before leaving on his journey (vv. 14-15)?

3. The master "entrusted" his property to the servants (v. 14). What does it mean to be entrusted with something?

4. What are some of the "talents" Jesus has entrusted to you?

5. Based on their actions, how do the servants differ in their understanding of what the master expects of them (vv. 16-18)?

6. Consider your daily schedule—how you invest the time, energy and abilities entrusted to you. Does your life more closely resemble the first two servants or the third? Explain.

7. When the master returns, how does he commend and reward the good and faithful servants (vv. 19-23)?

8. How does the third servant misunderstand the character of his master (vv. 24-27)?

9. What are the consequences of his wicked and lazy actions (vv. 28-30)?

10. If the wicked servant had known the end of the story, he might have acted differently. How should your life be different in light of Christ's coming to "settle accounts"?

11. What are some specific ways you might rearrange your schedule to be more faithful to what Jesus has entrusted to you?

[1]Oswald Sanders, *Spiritual Leadership* (Chicago: Moody Press, 1962), p. 88.

9
Guidance
2 Chronicles 20:1-30

All of us are faced with the constant need for guidance. What career should I pursue? Whom should I marry? Where should I live? Should I change jobs? In which church activity should I invest my time? How should I spend my weekend? From the major and critical questions of life to daily and mundane situations, we are bombarded by matters which demand a decision. Jehoshaphat, king of Judah from 870-845 B.C., found himself in the same position. He needed to discern God's direction in a time of crisis. In 2 Chronicles 20:1-30 we see principles of guidance which can help us to hear God's voice.

1. In what areas of your life do you presently need guidance?

2. Read 2 Chronicles 20:1-30. Describe the situation confronting Jehoshaphat (vv. 1-2).

Imagine yourself in a similar situation. What would you be feeling and thinking?

3. What is Jehoshaphat's immediate response (vv. 3-4)?

4. In Jehoshaphat's prayer, how does he perceive himself and God (vv. 5-12)?

5. Jehoshaphat's prayer evidences a knowledge of Scripture. How can Scripture help us in seeking guidance?

6. By what further means does God guide (vv. 13-17)?

Although such direct guidance is extraordinary, what principles of guidance can we learn from this prophecy?

7. In what ways does Jehoshaphat respond to the guidance he receives (vv. 18-21)?

8. How might you have responded? Why?

9. What is the result of Jehoshaphat's obedience to God's guidance (vv. 22-30)?

10. What principles about seeking God's guidance do we learn from Jehoshaphat's example?

11. How can you apply these principles in your current needs for guidance?

10
Worship
Revelation 4—5

W hat is God's ultimate purpose for men and women? To worship him! But to truly worship God we must see who he is and realize what he has done. In Revelation 4—5 we enter with the apostle John into the heavenly realms where we observe the response of those who truly see the Lord.

John is writing to believers around A.D. 90-95 during the reign of the emperor Domitian, a time of tremendous persecution. They were living in a world where evil was rampant and apparently all-powerful. However, John's focus on God in all his glory would have been an apt reminder that evil is not in control. God's purpose stands; *he* controls the world's destiny. The worship pictured in these chapters reorients our thinking too, giving us a vision of God's character and rule in the world.

1. What images come to mind when you think of worship?

2. Read chapter 4, imagining all that John experienced in his glimpse into heaven. Describe what he saw, heard and felt.

3. What is the first and primary sight which meets his eyes (vv. 2-3)?

What is the significance of this?

4. What do we learn about God's character from John's description in this chapter?

5. What response does this evoke from the four living creatures and the twenty-four elders (vv. 6-11)?

6. Read chapter 5. What characters are involved in verses 1-7, and what is the nature of their activity?

7. Jesus is described both as the "Lion of the tribe of Judah" (v. 5) and as "a Lamb, looking as if it had been slain" (v. 6). What do these names tell us about who Jesus is?

8. In verses 9-10, what do we learn about the results of Christ's death?

9. Reread verses 8-14, identifying the different beings worshiping the Lamb.

What different forms of worship do you see?

10. What does this variety suggest about our attitude toward forms of worship which are very different from what we are accustomed to?

11. Considering Revelation 4 and 5, how would you define worship?

12. Compare your worship with that of Revelation 4 and 5. What are the similarities and differences?

Why do you think this is so?

---

13. Considering God's character as seen in Revelation 4 and 5, spend some time now worshiping him in brief expressions of praise and thanksgiving.

11
Giving
1 Chronicles 29:1-20

M ark recounts an incident in which a crowd of affluent people are putting large amounts of money into the temple treasury. In stark contrast to such giving, a poverty-stricken widow comes forward and gives "all she had to live on." Jesus, watching the scene, strongly commends the widow for surpassing all the others in her giving (Mk 12:41-44). If Jesus were watching you put money into the "temple treasury," what would he say? 1 Chronicles 29:1-20 challenges us to consider our habits and our motives in giving.

1. What gives you the most satisfaction when you give money?

KNOWING I CAN HELP

2. Read 1 Chronicles 29:1-20. How does David demonstrate his devotion to the Lord God in the building of the temple (vv. 1-5)? RECOGNIZES PURPOSE. BY LEADING THE WAY IN GIVING NATIONAL & PERSONAL RESOURCES. CHALLENGED OTHERS

3. How does David's example affect the rest of the leadership of Israel (vv. 6-9)? THEY GAVE WILLINGLY & WHOLEHEARTED

4. How do your attitudes toward giving compare with those of Israel?

FIND MYSELF LACKING . WANT TO BUT LIVE BY SIGHT

5. What do you think it means to give "freely and wholeheartedly" (v. 9)?

WANT TO GIVE, NOT A BURDEN JOY & PRIVILEGE

6. For which of God's characteristics does David give him praise in verses 10-19?

GREATNESS SPLENDOR POWER EVERLASTING GLORY MAJESTY

How does God's character motivate him to give?

IT IS A DEMONSTRATION OF HIS POWER & LOVE

7. If we have difficulty giving "freely and wholeheartedly," what might this suggest about our understanding of God's character?

DON'T TRUST THAT GOD WILL

8. Contrast David's estimate of himself and his people with his description of God (vv. 14-20).

PEOPLE
- NOTHING
- GIVING WHAT HAS BEEN GIVEN

GOD
- EVERYTHING
- CREATOR OF ALL

9. What does David realize about possessions?

THEY ARE A BLESSING FROM GOD

How is this demonstrated?

GIVEN HONESTLY & WILLINGLY

10. Which possessions do you have trouble viewing as belonging to God?

In what ways do you cling to them?

11. Describe the relationship between worship and giving in this passage.

WORSHIP IS A NATURAL RESPONSE TO GIVING. GIVING IS AN INTEGRAL PART OF WORSHIP

How are they related in your life?

12. In verse 2 David writes, "With all my resources I have provided for the temple of my God." Considering the different types of resources God has entrusted to you (time, energy, money, car, house or apartment, books, records and so on), what would it mean for you to follow David's example?

12
Discipling
1 Thessalonians 2

Make disciples of all nations." These were among Jesus' last words to the disciples. In like manner Paul, shortly before his death, exhorted Timothy to train faithful men who would in turn train others. This command is as critical today as it was for the church in the first century. But what does it mean to make disciples? Paul's own life provides a superb example.

In Acts 17:1-9 we learn that Paul, Silas and Timothy established the church at Thessalonica. However, they were forced to leave after only a few weeks due to persecution by the Jews. Because of Paul's concern for these new believers, he sent Timothy back to encourage them. After Timothy's return, Paul wrote the letter of 1 Thessalonians to them.

1. Think of a more mature Christian who influenced you toward godliness. What did you learn from his or her example?

2. Read 1 Thessalonians 2. What were Paul's motives in sharing the gospel with the Thessalonians (vv. 1-6)?

3. How does this compare with your motivation for giving yourself to other people?

4. What metaphors does Paul use to describe his care for the Thessalonians (vv. 7-12)?

How does each of these enhance our understanding of his relationship with them?

5. What was Paul's goal for them (2:12; see also 3:12-13)?

6. In what specific ways did it cost Paul to invest his life in the Thessalonians?

How are the costs similar for us today?

7. What were the results of Paul's labors in the lives of the Thessalonians (vv. 13-16)?

8. Why will the Thessalonian Christians be Paul's hope, joy and crown when the Lord Jesus returns (vv. 17-20)?

9. How can Paul's example help us invest in the lives of other Christians?

10. What younger Christians has God placed around you?

In light of Paul's example, how can you influence them toward godliness?

11. Give thanks for those people who have had a godly influence on you. Pray for specific individuals in whom you can invest your life.

Leader's Notes

Leading a Bible discussion can be an enjoyable and rewarding experience. But it can also be *scary*—especially if you've never done it before. If this is your feeling, you're in good company. When God asked Moses to lead the Israelites out of Egypt, he replied, "O Lord, please send someone else to do it!" (Ex 4:13).

When Solomon became king of Israel, he felt the task was far beyond his abilities. "I am only a little child and do not know how to carry out my duties. . . . Who is able to govern this great people of yours?" (1 Kings 3:7, 9).

When God called Jeremiah to be a prophet, he replied, "Ah, Sovereign LORD, . . . I do not know how to speak; I am only a child" (Jer 1:6).

The list goes on. The apostles were "unschooled, ordinary men" (Acts 4:13). Timothy was young, frail and frightened. Paul's "thorn in the flesh" made him feel weak. But God's response to all of his servants—including you—is essentially the same: "My grace is sufficient for you" (2 Cor 12:9). Relax. God helped these people in spite of their weaknesses, and he can help you in spite of your feelings of inadequacy.

There is another reason why you should feel encouraged. Leading a Bible discussion is not difficult if you follow certain guidelines. You don't need to be an expert on the Bible or a trained teacher. The suggestions listed below should enable you to effectively and enjoyably fulfill your role as leader.

Preparing to Lead

1. Ask God to help you understand and apply the passage to your own life. Unless this happens, you will not be prepared to lead others. Pray too for the various members of the group. Ask God to give you an enjoyable and profitable time together studying his Word.

2. As you begin each study, read and reread the assigned Bible passage to familiarize yourself with what the author is saying. In the case of book studies, you may want to read through the entire book prior to the first study. This will give you a helpful overview of its contents.

3. This study guide is based on the New International Version of the Bible. It will help you and the group if you use this translation as the basis for your study and discussion. Encourage others to use the NIV also, but allow them the freedom to use whatever translation they prefer.

4. Carefully work through each question in the study. Spend time in meditation and reflection as you formulate your answers.

5. Write your answers in the space provided in the study guide. This will help you to express your understanding of the passage clearly.

6. It might help you to have a Bible dictionary handy. Use it to look up any unfamiliar words, names or places. (For additional help on how to study a passage, see chapter five of *Leading Bible Discussions,* IVP.)

7. Once you have finished your own study of the passage, familiarize yourself with the leader's notes for the study you are leading. These are designed to help you in several ways. First, they tell you the purpose the study guide author had in mind while writing the study. Take time to think through how the study questions work together to accomplish that purpose. Second, the notes provide you with additional background information or comments on some of the questions. This information can be useful if people have difficulty understanding or answering a question. Third, the leader's notes can alert you to potential problems you may encounter during the study.

8. If you wish to remind yourself of anything mentioned in the leader's notes, make a note to yourself below that question in the study.

Leading the Study

1. Begin the study on time. Unless you are leading an evangelistic Bible study, open with prayer, asking God to help you to understand and apply the passage.

2. Be sure that everyone in your group has a study guide. Encourage them to prepare beforehand for each discussion by working through the questions in the guide.

3. At the beginning of your first time together, explain that these studies are meant to be discussions not lectures. Encourage the members of the group to participate. However, do not put pressure on those who may be hesitant to speak during the first few sessions.

4. Read the introductory paragraph at the beginning of the discussion. This will orient the group to the passage being studied.

5. Read the passage aloud if you are studying one chapter or less. You may choose to do this yourself, or someone else may read if he or she has been asked to do so prior to the study. Longer passages may occasionally be read in parts at different times during the study. Some studies may cover several chapters. In such cases reading aloud would probably take too much time, so the group members should simply read the assigned passages prior to the study.

6. As you begin to ask the questions in the guide, keep several things in mind. First, the questions are designed to be used just as they are written. If you wish, you may simply read them aloud to the group. Or you may prefer to express them in your own words. However, unnecessary rewording of the questions is not recommended.

Second, the questions are intended to guide the group toward understanding and applying the *main idea* of the passage. The author of the guide has stated his or her view of this central idea in the *purpose* of the study in the leader's notes. You should try to understand how the passage expresses this idea and how the study questions work together to lead the group in that direction.

There may be times when it is appropriate to deviate from the study guide. For example, a question may have already been answered. If so, move on to the next question. Or someone may raise an important question not covered in the guide. Take time to discuss it! The important thing is to use discretion. There may be many routes you can travel to reach the goal of the study. But the easiest route is usually the one the author has suggested.

7. Avoid answering your own questions. If necessary, repeat or rephrase them until they are clearly understood. An eager group quickly becomes passive and silent if they think the leader will do most of the talking.

8. Don't be afraid of silence. People may need time to think about the question before formulating their answers.

9. Don't be content with just one answer. Ask, "What do the rest of you think?" or "Anything else?" until several people have given answers to the question.

10. Acknowledge all contributions. Try to be affirming whenever possible. Never reject an answer. If it is clearly wrong, ask, "Which verse led you to that conclusion?" or again, "What do the rest of you think?"

11. Don't expect every answer to be addressed to you, even though this will probably happen at first. As group members become more at ease, they will begin to truly interact with each other. This is one sign of a healthy discussion.

12. Don't be afraid of controversy. It can be very stimulating. If you don't resolve an issue completely, don't be frustrated. Move on and keep it in mind for later. A subsequent study may solve the problem.

13. Stick to the passage under consideration. It should be the source for answering the questions. Discourage the group from unnecessary cross-referencing. Likewise, stick to the subject and avoid going off on tangents.

14. Periodically summarize what the *group* has said about the passage. This helps to draw together the various ideas mentioned and gives continuity to the study. But don't preach.

15. Conclude your time together with conversational prayer. Be sure to ask God's help to apply those things which you learned in the study.

16. End on time.

Many more suggestions and helps are found in *Leading Bible Discussions* (IVP). Reading and studying through that would be well worth your time.

Components of Small Groups

A healthy small group should do more than study the Bible. There are four components you should consider as you structure your time together.

Nurture. Being a part of a small group should be a nurturing and edifying experience. You should grow in your knowledge and love of God and each other. If we are to properly love God, we must know and keep his commandments (Jn 14:15). That is why Bible study should be a foundational part of your small group. But you can be nurtured by other things as well. You can memorize Scripture, read and discuss a book, or occasionally listen to a tape of a good speaker.

Community. Most people have a need for close friendships. Your small group can be an excellent place to cultivate such relationships. Allow time for informal interaction before and after the study. Have a time of sharing during the meeting. Do fun things together as a group, such as a potluck supper or a picnic. Have someone bring refreshments to the meeting. Be creative!

Worship. A portion of your time together can be spent in worship and prayer. Praise God together for who he is. Thank him for what he has done and is doing in your lives and in the world. Pray for each other's needs. Ask God to help you to apply what you have learned. Sing hymns together.

Mission. Many small groups decide to work together in some form of outreach. This can be a practical way of applying what you have learned. You can host a series of evangelistic discussions for your friends or neighbors. You can visit people at a home for the elderly. Help a widow with cleaning or repair jobs around her home. Such projects can have a transforming influence on your group.

For a detailed discussion of the nature and function of small groups, read *Small Group Leaders' Handbook* or *Good Things Come in Small Groups* (both from IVP).

Study 1. Quiet Time. Exodus 33:7—34:10, 27-35.
Purpose: To reflect on how Moses' experience with God can give us practical help for our quiet times.

Question 1. Almost every study begins with an "approach" question, which is meant to be asked *before* the passage is read. These questions are important for several reasons.

First, they help the group to warm up to each other. No matter how well a group may know each other or how comfortable they may be with each other, there is always a stiffness that needs to be overcome before people will begin to talk openly. A good question will break the ice.

Second, approach questions get people thinking along the lines of the topic of the study. Most people will have lots of different things going on in their minds (dinner, an important meeting coming up, how to get the car fixed) that will have nothing to do with the study. A creative question will get their attention and draw them into the discussion.

Third, approach questions can reveal where our thoughts or feelings need to be transformed by Scripture. This is why it is especially important *not* to read the passage before the approach question is asked. The passage will tend to color the honest reactions people would otherwise give because they are of course *supposed* to think the way the Bible does. Giving honest responses to various issues before they find out what the Bible says may help them to see where their thoughts or attitudes need to be changed.

Question 2. The "tent of meeting" was a temporary meeting place of God and his people.

Question 4. While it may seem simple, this is a very important question. Don't settle for merely observational answers. Be ready to help the group to grasp how truly startling (and unlike us today) were Moses' requests. These verses expose Moses' deep hunger to know God "as the deer pants for streams of water" (Ps 42:1). This, after all, is the essential ingredient of a quiet time. Without this a quiet time easily degenerates into legalism.

Question 10. Four elements of a quiet time can be noted here: worship, petition, confession and listening to God speak (that is, Bible study). While it will be helpful to observe these things, they should in no way be imposed as laws for daily quiet time.

Question 13. In 2 Corinthians 3:18 Paul writes, "And we, who with unveiled faces all reflect the Lord's glory, are being transformed into his likeness with ever-increasing glory, which comes from the Lord, who is the Spirit." Paul uses the experience of Moses to illustrate the transforming work of the Spirit in our lives.

Study 2. Prayer. Nehemiah 1:1—2:10.
Purpose: To consider what Nehemiah's example can teach us about prayer.

Question 2. In verse 11 Nehemiah mentions that he was "cupbearer to the king." His job was to taste the king's wine in order to insure against poisoning. Cupbearers were normally foreigners, but they occupied a high position and often had considerable influence with the king. This may explain why his brother and the men from Judah came to him.

Question 5. Nehemiah's use of the third person plural in confession stands in sharp contrast to the individualistic approach which typifies most contemporary Christians. You may want to highlight this point.

Question 6. Nehemiah is quoting from Deuteronomy 30:2-4 in his prayer.

Question 8. Some members of your group may not understand the meaning of *consecration* or *supplication. Consecration* means to dedicate ourselves to God's service. *Supplication* means to ask for something humbly and earnestly.

Question 10. The mention of the month Nisan in 2:1 indicates that it was four months since the news had reached Nehemiah. This fact, in conjunction with the phrases *for some days* (1:4) and *day and night* (1:6), are further indication of a diligent and persevering prayer life.

Nehemiah had good reason to be afraid (2:2). Rulers at that time could punish or even execute a servant for being sad in their presence. Also, Artaxerxes had previously halted the rebuilding of Jerusalem because it was considered a place of rebellion and sedition (Ezra 4:18-22). In asking him to rescind this order, Nehemiah risked being identified as a rebel.

Study 3. Bible Study. 2 Kings 22:1—23:7, 21-25.
Purpose: To realize the serious consequences of neglecting God's Word and the transforming effect it can have when studied and obeyed.

Question 3. The Book of the Law was probably the book of Deuteronomy or a substantial portion of it. It was read twice in one day, and many of the reforms are closely related to material in Deuteronomy.

If people don't know the meaning of *ironic,* tell them irony is a contrast between what might be expected and what actually occurs.

Question 9. In the book of Kings, Josiah and his great-grandfather Hezekiah are the only kings who receive God's unqualified approval.

Question 10. Encourage the group to give examples of how Scripture has made a significant impact on their lives and relationships. Positive and practical examples here will reinforce the teaching of the passage.

Question 11. You may want to suggest some resources for Bible study and memorization. IVP publishes a number of other study guides for individual and group use. For Scripture memory, you might recommend *Scripture Memory 101* (IVP) and the *Topical Memory System* (NavPress).

Study 4. Evangelism. Acts 17.
Purpose: To learn from Paul some principles for effectively sharing the gospel.

Question 1. Spend only a brief time on this question as it will be considered more fully in the rest of the study.

Question 5. Our evangelism should always be based on the Bible. But often we can't start there because it is meaningless to many people. In such cases we may need to meet them with something from their own background.

Question 8. The marketplace *(agora)* was the center of Athenian life and activity.

In the first century, Epicureanism was primarily a philosophy of the educated upper classes. They downplayed the existence of spiritual realities, emphasizing only the material world. The goal of their lives was true happiness attained by moderation and detachment from the world. The Stoics, although more spiritually oriented, also sought a life of serene detachment.

Question 11. Paul and Jesus explained the gospel differently to different types of people (for example, Jesus' conversation with Nicodemus was different from his talk with the rich young ruler). Likewise, our presentation of the gospel must be tailored to the understanding and background of our listener. However, all of us need to have a handle on the basic facts of the gospel message. Memorizing a gospel outline is a good way to begin.

"In ancient Athens there was a council which used to meet on the *Areopagus,* a hill overlooking the *agora,* and which still retained its importance as the chief court in Athens in the first century. . . . The reference to Dionysius the Areopagite (verse 34) . . . suggests that Luke meant to describe a meeting of the court, no doubt in public session and not necessarily taking the form of a legal trial" (I. Howard Marshall, *Acts,* in the Tyndale New Testament

Commentaries, ed. Leon Morris [Grand Rapids, Mich.: Eerdmans, 1980], pp. 284-85).

Question 13. The purpose of this question is to allow the group to sum-marize the principles of evangelism learned from this passage.

Study 5. Social Justice. Amos 5:4—6:7.

Purpose: To see the biblical call to justice and mercy and to begin to live out these elements of the Christian life.

Question 2. During the divided kingdom, Jeroboam, king of Israel, feared that the temple in Jerusalem would draw his people to give their allegiance to Rehoboam, king of Judah. Therefore, he set up golden calves in Bethel and Dan (1 Kings 12:25-33). By the time of Amos, Gilgal and Beersheba had also become centers of the false religious cult of Israel (Amos 5:5-6).

Question 7. Shortly after Amos spoke, his prophecies came to pass. Assyria crushed the northern kingdom, taking thousands into exile.

Question 8. Some have misunderstood the meaning of 5:21-27, assuming that the Lord rejected all formal religious worship. God desires worship, but only when it is coupled with justice and righteousness.

Questions 9-11. These questions are somewhat controversial and may elicit a wide variety of responses. Be sensitive to people who may be feeling overwhelmed by their guilt or the magnitude of injustice in the world. It may be helpful to have some resources and avenues available for follow-up such as those offered through World Vision and Bread for the World.

Study 6. The Church. Ephesians 4:1-16.

Purpose: To understand the nature and purpose of a healthy church and our own place within the church.

Question 2. The Greek verb for *make every effort* (v. 3) is in the present tense, emphasizing that our efforts toward unity require continuous and dil-igent action.

Question 4. You might ask the group to consider how each of the "ones" Paul mentions provides a basis for unity.

Question 5. Paul, quoting Psalm 68:18, turns from a focus on the unity of the church to its diversity. Jesus has descended and ascended to the right hand of the Father in glory. From this position of authority and power he bestows gifts of the Spirit to the body in order that it might become mature (see John Stott, *The Message of Ephesians* [IVP, 1979], p. 155-59).

Question 7. Don't be content with a verbatim repetition of Paul's words. Encourage the group to put the answer in their own words.

Questions 13-14. After you discuss these questions, you may want to enter into a time of praise for God's creation of a new society. Praise him for the diversity of the body and the various gifts he has distributed among his people. Be sure to evaluate the group's commitment to live out the vision of the church which has been presented in Ephesians 4:1-16.

Study 7. Missions/Crosscultural Ministry. Acts 10.

Purpose: To see that God's concern for the world compels us to cross cultural and geographical barriers with the message of Christ.

Question 2. It is fun to read this chapter dramatically. Ask members of the group to read the parts of the narrator, the angel, Cornelius, the heavenly voice and Peter.

Question 3. It is interesting to note that God used a vision with Peter rather than communicating with him directly, as in verses 19-20. You might ask the group why a vision would have made a greater impact on Peter.

Question 8. The fact that God does not show favoritism may seem obvious to us. Peter too had heard Jesus expound this theme. However, transferring this head knowledge into heart knowledge was as difficult for Peter as it is for us.

Question 9. Caesarea, the home of Cornelius, was north of Jerusalem, Judea and Samaria. It was in the category of "the ends of the earth."

Note that Jerusalem and Judea shared the same language and culture as the disciples; Samaria shared the same language and a similar but also different culture; the ends of the earth represent different languages and cultures.

Question 10. Peter's thoughts about the status of the Gentiles are recorded in Acts 11:15-17. He and the other Jews were surprised that the Holy Spirit was given to the Gentiles. They evidently assumed that this gift was reserved for Jews.

Question 14. In summary you may want to tie together the themes of missions and crosscultural ministry.

Study 8. Managing Time and Gifts. Matthew 25:14-30.

Purpose: To manage our time and use our gifts effectively in light of Christ's lordship and imminent return.

Question 2. This parable falls within the broader context of Jesus' discussion of his second coming and the nature of the kingdom of heaven. The Parable of the Talents illustrates one aspect of the kingdom of heaven.

Questions 3-4. A talent was not a coin but a measure or weight of money. Its value varied according to the metal being weighed. The number of talents given to the different men was dependent upon their ability (v. 15).

In current English usage the word *talent* refers to a person's own natural ability or aptitude. In this parable, however, the talents belong to someone else.

Question 6. We normally speak of *our* time, money and gifts. This may be quite natural, but it may also betray a serious misunderstanding. These things—including our very lives—are not our own but have been entrusted to us by God.

Question 8. Be careful not to spend too much time on this question. It is not central to the parable.

Question 9. If the servant had merely been stripped of his responsibilities, Jesus' words would not seem so ominous. But in fact the servant was cast "into the darkness, where there will be weeping and gnashing of teeth" (v. 30). This is not a loss of reward but rather an exclusion from the kingdom of heaven. It is well to note, however, that the wicked servant had done *nothing* with his talent. His life was totally unmotivated by the master's imminent return. His response is not the result of weak faith, but unbelief.

Study 9. Guidance. 2 Chronicles 20:1-30.

Purpose: To understand biblical principles of guidance, demonstrated by their application to one specific situation.

Question 2. This attack may have been a judgment against Jehoshaphat for helping the king of Israel (see 19:2).

Question 5. Jehoshaphat does not quote from Scripture, but his prayer reflects a knowledge of God's past dealings and promises to Israel.

Question 6. God guides in a wide variety of ways. Scripture records God guiding through his Word (Lk 4:1-13), through wise counsel (2 Sam 16:23), circumstances (1 Cor 16:8-9), dreams (Mt 1:20-25), visions (Acts 16:6-10), drawing of lots (Acts 1:23-26), and so on. Some of these methods of guidance, such as Scripture, are normative. Others, such as dreams and visions, tend to be the exception. While we can always expect God to guide, we cannot presume to know how he will guide us.

Question 11. You may want to conclude the study by having individuals share specific needs for guidance in their lives. Spend time praying for one another.

In your summary you may want to share this helpful insight from John White's *The Fight* (IVP): "First, God has an overall goal for your life; second, God's goal is a moral goal. His supreme object is to make you like his Son (Rom 8:29). Whether the process of making what he wants of you involves travel, money, joy, pain or whatever is secondary. His goal is to make you holy, and the kind of guidance he will give you will reflect this" (p. 156).

Study 10. Worship. Revelation 4—5.
Purpose: To see God's worthiness and to worship him.

Question 2. A lot is happening here. You might suggest that one person in the group read the chapter aloud while the others close their eyes and listen. This has proven effective in enabling people to enter into the scene being described. Encourage the group to use their imagination.

Question 4. Don't stop with those attributes of God which are expressly stated in the passage. Help the group to probe more deeply into the signif-icance of the imagery used. What do these different images suggest about God's character?

Question 5. It would be easy to give a one-word answer here. Move people beyond the obvious by having them focus on the content of the worship.

Question 6. Imagination continues to be crucial to getting the full impact of the passage.

Questions 9-10. These questions can be very significant in helping the group develop a healthy attitude toward worship. Be sure they notice in particular those forms of worship which are quite uncharacteristic of what they are used to (for example, the burning of incense). Try to create an open, accepting atmosphere so that people feel free to share their own experiences and different traditions. Your aim is to help individuals appreciate diversity in worship and see their need to be open to the Holy Spirit's leading in a variety of ways. Be prepared to spend time on these questions.

Question 12. If this question has been fully considered in your discussion of questions 8-9, feel free to skip it. You may want to highlight significant points in your summary.

Question 13. Encourage participation in this time of worship. Emphasize the word *brief* so that everyone in the group will feel free to contribute, especially if the group is unaccustomed to such unstructured times of wor-ship. You might also sing a worshipful hymn.

Study 11. Giving. 1 Chronicles 29:1-20.
Purpose: To realize that all we have comes from God and to give wisely and generously.

Question 2. Have the group carefully observe everything in these first five verses so they will realize the extent to which David's devotion drove him.

Question 5. It is important to see that for David giving was not a burden or an unfortunate responsibility, but rather a joy and privilege in light of God's tremendous grace.

Question 10. The answers to this question are foundational for a renewed attitude toward giving. Be ready to draw people out, not only in terms of their habits and struggles with money but also with respect to other possessions which they may have in greater abundance.

Question 12. Move people to be specific and practical in answering this question.

Study 12. Discipling. 1 Thessalonians 2.

Purpose: To understand and begin to apply the biblical mandate to make disciples.

Question 1. Encourage several people to contribute here. This can be a very uplifting discussion as people remember those whom God has significantly used in their lives. Help them focus not only on ways they were formally taught by more mature Christians, but also on the ways they were influenced by casual times with godly Christian friends. This will encourage even the less mature or less confident members of your group to see that they too can significantly influence others.

Question 4. This question is important for cultivating a right attitude toward discipling. Be sure the group observes that Paul did not see the Thessalonian Christians simply as a "project." He was motivated by deep love for them and for Christ, and a sincere desire to see them mature in their relationship with him. This will be crucial for their own investment in the lives of others.

Question 10. Encourage people to be specific. You may want to direct their thinking to the things they appreciated about those who influenced them (question 1). They might be able to do these same things for others.

Andrea Sterk, a former InterVarsity campus staff member, is pursuing Ph.D. studies in church history. Peter Scazzero, also a former InterVarsity staff member, is pastor of New Life Fellowship Church in New York City.